PAINTING WITH WORDS - A POETRY COLLECTION

Cathy McGough

Stratford Living Publishing

Copyright © 2013 by Cathy McGough
All rights reserved.
Originally published under the title Painting With Words (25 poems.)
This updated Poetry Collection published in July, 2024, (70 poems.)
No portion of this book may be reproduced in any form without written permission from the publisher or author, except as permitted by U.S. copyright law without prior permission in writing from the Publisher at Stratford Living Publishing.
ISBN PAPERBACK: 978-1-998480-14-2
Cathy McGough has asserted her right under the Copyright, Designs and Patents Act, 1988 to be identified as the author of this work.
Cover art powered by Canva Pro.
This is a work of fiction. The characters and situations are all fictional. Resemblance to any persons living or dead is purely coincidental. Names, characters, places, and incidents are either the products of the author's imagination or are used fictitiously.

Contents

Dedication	VII
CASTLES IN THE AIR	1
THIS TO BRING YOU BACK	3
WORKADAY	5
BLUE JAYS AND KOOKABURRAS	7
EVERYTHING BUT LOVE	9
PERSONIFICATION	11
THE PAPER DOLL	12
YOU AWAKEN WHILE I SLEEP	13
FOOD FOR THE MUSE	15
CURTAIN OF MIST	16
LAST DANCE	17
I CAN FLY	18

ON THE SURFACE	20
PRETTY LITTLE THING	21
CRUCI-FICTION	23
RESURRECTION	25
THE TEASE	26
THE BEGINNING	27
WHY ME?	28
THE TREE	29
THE EYES OF HEAVEN	30
THE FINAL STAGE	32
SONG FROM THE SEA	33
THE PAINTER WHO WOULD NEVER BE	35
BEAUTEOUS SUNSET	37
BOYS WITH TOYS	39
ONE OF THOSE DAYS...	41
THE ART OF PARENTING	43
STEAMY	44
THE ICY HAND OF TIME	45
SONG OF AUTUMN	47
THE CIRCLE: A TRILOGY	48
THE CIRCLE A TRILOGY:	50

THE CIRCLE: A TRILOGY	51
THE MARRIAGE PRAYER	53
BEAU IDEAL	55
FATHER AND SON	56
FLEETING	57
FORGET ME NOT CHILD	58
HANDS	59
HE LOVES ME	61
IGNORAMOUS	62
PUT A BANDAID	63
IF I COULD...	65
MIRROR MIRROR	67
ORGAN GRINDERS	68
REFLECTIONS IN A MUD PUDDLE	70
SHACKLED TOGETHER	72
SIGN OF THE TIMES	74
THE ANSWER	76
DEATH OF A SNOWFLAKE	78
THE PAST	79
THE UNSPOKEN	80
WATERMELON LADY	81

HEARTLESS	83
PASSOVER	85
TAKEN TOO SOON	87
WHISPER	88
SCARAMOUCHE	90
WALKING DOWN THE PATH	92
BARRIER	94
SLIGHT MISUNDERSTANDING	97
MACBETH	98
PERHAPS	100
SIPHON	102
UNANSWERABLE LETTERS	103
BUTTERFLY	105
EVOLUTION	106
THE WORLD IN 60 SECONDS	108
GOSPELAMER	111
Acknowlegements	113
About Cathy	115
Also by:	117

For Mom and Dad

CASTLES IN THE AIR

I build you like a tower
And then close you down
There are too many windows
It's too far to the ground.
You sit upon your pedestal
Repelling every single force
Because you see me as a shadow
Of your mother's divorce.
And it may be less than love
And it may be more than most
But it is something, growing stronger.
I read you like a book
Your pages fly open wide
Without a glance or look
It seems our spirits confide
And it may be less than love
And it may be more than most
But it is something, growing deeper
It may not be the kind of love
That will last and last forever

But I'd rather have a part of love
Than to have none what-so-ever.

THIS TO BRING YOU BACK

Faces, passing in and out of mind
   Memories of stars, which have shined
   Openings and closings
   Crowded solitudes
   Who are these people?
   A child appears in the flower of youth
   Pressing her face to the window
   She wonders what is the truth
   Her attention seems to falter
   When she eyes the candy all about her
   And wonders if they are free.
   Child, didn't your mama tell you
   That nothing comes for free
   Everything has a price
   Everyone has a price to pay.
   Faces, dreams of olden times
   All fade and form into new rhymes
   As we follow in the footsteps
   Of our deceased heroes

Seeking out faces
Which are non-existent

WORKADAY

Dismal enclosure
  Padded
  Purple walls
  Boxed in
  Prisoner.
  Tried to get released
  On parole
  But fell back in
  Before I could
  Pull myself out
  In this place
  There are machines
  Who talk you into
  Working
  As a machine
  And when you refuse
  They break you down
  You break down
  "Listen keyboard
  Without me
  You're nothing!

Nothing I say!

Just remember that
Ok then. Ok."

Wire-less mouse
Seizes
Opportunity
To escape
Jumps &
Plops into
Extra extra large
Mug of java.

Steaming
Streaming
SCREAMING!
Little Fire
Ooops!

BLUE JAYS AND KOOKABURRAS

It doesn't matter if I don't know the name of every flower
  It doesn't matter if I don't know the name of every bird
  Being a newcomer to this land does not deter me
  From praising with both deeds and words.
  Sometimes it feels almost like home to me
  Wandering aimlessly with no ties to the past
  On other days it feels like this island is my soul
  And I wonder if this infatuation will last.
  Then there are days when I feel like a betrayer
  Longing for things I can no longer attain
  Then a glimpse of the flag from my homeland
  Beckons me back once again.
  So what is it, when you are born somewhere
  Can you ever entirely leave that place behind?
  Or can you love the new and love the old
  In your heart, as well as in your mind?
  Soon cotton-ball clouds will part for my silvery bird
  My first love awaits with arms open wide

White Trilliums will smother me in their fragrant kisses
As Blue Jays and Kookaburras collide.

EVERYTHING BUT LOVE

You gave me flowers
  You gave me candy
  But that wasn't enough.
  You took me driving
  To high class places
  But that wasn't enough.
  You gave me everything
  That you could think of
  Everything but love
  Yes, everything but love.
  You told me jokes
  You made me laugh
  But that wasn't enough.
  You gave me time
  You gave me space
  But that wasn't enough.
  You gave me everything
  That you could think of
  Everything but love
  Everything but love.
  How long I waited for a tender kiss

For a sign, a proposal or a ring
But day after day, year after year
1 + 1 added up to nothing.

You told me jokes
You made me laugh
But that wasn't enough.
You gave me time
You gave me space
But that wasn't enough.7
You gave me everything
That you could think of
When all I wanted was your love
Dear, all I really wanted was your love

PERSONIFICATION

Spinning around you
   Like a top
   Recklessly
   Bouncing from wall to wall
   Self-destructing
   But plodding onward
   Not taking time to think
   Or gasp for air
   Walls changing positions
   Like scenes from a home movie
   Colours blending
   Running wild
   Ceiling flies over and under
   And blends in with the floor
   Like a child with a kaleidoscope
   You change the frame
   Taking pleasure in my song
   Until I unwind
   And escape through the ceiling
   Into a more meaningful relationship

THE PAPER DOLL

The paper doll is tangled in the whirl of the wind
    Drained of emotion she twirls and she spins
    Around and around, ballerina-like pirouettes
    Flashing back to life's failures and regrets.
    Frantically trying from its clutches to escape
    In her ears the wind is whispering rape.
    The paper doll is torn from limb to limb
    A mere memory of what could have been.
    She feels no pain for she is only a child
    She feels nothing.
    Hear the cry of the children as they toss and turn
    In the dreams of their sleep
    Protect them from the whirlwinds of life.

    Run, children run,
    There are no chains to bind you any longer.
    Protect them from the whirlwinds of life.

YOU AWAKEN WHILE I SLEEP

You awaken while I sleep
  Pack your suitcases
  Kiss me on the cheek
  You softly whisper "goodbye"
  I watch you go
  Though you will never know
  For in your eyes
  I sleep peacefully
  Turning my back to your empty space
  Tears, sobs, pitying myself
  Sleep is welcomed

  My spirit seeks yours out
  They play tag together
  Our love is how it use to be
  I am you. You are me.
  The sun brings in the morning
  I reach toward your empty space
  I am enveloped in your embrace

Love brought you back today
Love brought you back to stay.

You awaken while I sleep
Pack your suitcases
Kiss me on the cheek
You softly whisper "goodbye"
I lock the door. I fasten the chain.
This scene will never play again.

FOOD FOR THE MUSE

Come to me my beautiful leaf
  Fall into my waiting embrace
  Bathe me in your running colour
  Flutter to me in grace.
  Leaf they call you soul-less
  I say that this is wrong
  Because you dance in harmony
  While the wind plays your song.
  Now I take you in my arms and weep
  At the bleeding of your veins
  Colour running into colour: beauty
  These are your remains.

  Crunchy chatter-box companion
  Tickling soles of shoes
  Autumnal inspiration:
  Food for the muse.

CURTAIN OF MIST

Through the thickened mist
  I saw a pair of marble eyes
  Reflecting nothing they hissed
  Reclining into their disguise
  Stars fell just like snow
  Into their strong perception
  Captivated by their glow
  I walked in their direction.
  Unfeeling and hollow were they
  Transmitting their silent ray
  Through the endless mist I saw
  The moonlight had begun to thaw
  I raised my arms to catch the truth
  Judgment came, I lost my youth.
  All of my emotions being drained
  In the morning there remained
  Under the clear and grey blue skies
  Two pairs of marble eyes.

LAST DANCE

Holding your picture in my arms
Dancing together across the floor
Almost the way it could have been
If only you had only loved me more
Close enough to feel your heartbeat
Swirling together in an imaginary cloud
Painting the world in a brilliant sheen
Whispering your name out loud.
Dancing, though the music has ended
With tears streaming down my face
For I have seen what could have been
And have lost it without a trace.

I CAN FLY

Standing at the edge
   Wailing winds
   Fluttering sleeves
   Ever ready
   Needing
   Solo flight
   Skirts rippling
   Left foot back
   Right foot forward
   Poised
   Look Angels
   Just there
   Copper hair floating
   Lips tasting
   Sea salt
   Taking it all
   In
   Knowing
   Who I am
   Why I am here
   Wings

Fluttering
Beat beat beating
I know
That I must
Soar.

For
I live on
The edge
Of imagination
Where feet
No longer desire
The ground
I see
All
From a unique
Perspective
I am a poet
An Author
And
I can fly.

ON THE SURFACE

Mirror,
   You reflect me with redundancy
   Written all over me
   Is flesh coloured uncertainty.
   Mirror,
   You mock perfection
   With this unrefrained reflection
   And the result is always the same
   In your frame: I remain unchanged.
   Written between the lines
   Disguised poetically
   Inescapable features
   Flow inharmoniously.
   Mirror: I adhere to what I see
   For I am you, through and through
   But sometimes reflection
   I wish that I resembled you.

PRETTY LITTLE THING

Pretty little thing
  Sits ornamentally
  Greeting all who enter
  With utmost cordiality.
  She's the prettiest girl
  They have ever seen
  With her golden locks
  And her eyes of green.
  She is a china doll
  Brought to life
  Someday she will make some man
  A wonderful wife.
  Pretty little thing
  Smiles angelically
  Singing nursery rhymes
  For her parents' company
  She only speaks
  When she is spoken to
  She never thinks -
  Has no reason to
  She is as pretty as a picture

Would put Mona Lisa to shame
And this child of a woman
Plays the etiquette game.
Pretty little thing
Never questions
Her parents' propriety
Because all she has ever been
Was an Angel
Upon their Christmas tree.

CRUCI-FICTION

Your body is bound
In the shape of a cross
You hang there in despair
For all of eternity.
They would have mended
Your hands and feet
But the nails were rusting
And tetanus shots
Had yet to be invented.
They would have healed
Your sides
But when they stood
Beside you and looked
Through the gaping hole
The view of the world
through your soul
Was breath-taking.
They would have removed
The crown
But the blood stains

Fell down your forehead
Forming shapes
Like delicate
Rose petals.

Moving from station to station
Tightening my grip
On the black rosary
It breaks
Beads roll everywhere:21
Under the pews
In the aisles.
I genuflect
As I pick up each tiny
Black rose petal
Then gather them up
Into my hat.
Outside
The wind catches them
Lifting them
Skyward
Black crows
Soaring out of reach
Dropping blankets
On the homeless
The believers
The non-believers
And me.

RESURRECTION

Drifting into emptiness
   Spreading like a rumour
   Leaf floats down the stream
   Ghostly presence from a dream.
   Leaf crushed and broken
   Washes up on shore
   Sugar-coated by sand
   Lifeless evermore.
   Leaf dries and is re-born
   Lifted by an angel's breath
   Gabriel blows his horn
   Leaf after death.

THE TEASE

He asked me and I said "I can't"
  He asked me and I said "I shan't"
  He asks me every day. He asks me every night.
  He sticks around hoping, that one day I just might.
  I'm stalling and only I know why.
  I'm not on a power trip! Oh no, not I!
  Because I do so hate to hurt my guy.
  It's not easy to see a grown man cry.
  Still, I have to turn him down.
  Still, I have to see him frown.
  Still, I have faith that he will stay.
  (I think he loves me by the way.)
  One day I will be sure.
  One day the timing will be right.
  I will open up my heart to him
  And darkness will turn into light.
  I hope all of this secrecy
  Will not ruin our future. You see:
  This stalling isn't purely by chance
  He's like Astaire and I can't dance.

THE BEGINNING

I sat
  Under a blanket of darkness
  There was a beclouding
  That just would not lift.
  Love,
  Had grown cold in your heart
  But when you told me
  I was too confused
  To realize that you were trying to tell me
  The truth.
  Now,
  All alone
  At the edge of the woods
  I sing.
  My spirit reaches out
  I sing
  Until the voice echoes
  And I remember
  That this was "our song"
  And the healing begins.

WHY ME?

The chorus plays repeatedly
   Interrupting internal harmony
   As fantasy with unblushing charms
   Sends my love into another's arms.
   Memories shattered on the ground
   Voices muffled by recessive frowns
   Whispers, confusion yet c'est la vie
   Adjusting to life's calm reality.
   Oh the rain is never-ending
   And the breeze is forever sending
   It's empathetic messages to me.
   In an uncertain tomorrow
   The pitter-patter of droplets
   Will pierce my ears with silence
   And tears will leave me stone-cold
   At the end of the rainbow
   Hoarding my pot of gold.

THE TREE

How many years
  How long, how old?
  Tree surgeons ponder,
  Buds of knowledge unfold.
  Grasping for tomorrow
  To the god of all creation
  Angelic fingers reaching out
  In wooden motivation.
  Plant and replant,
  Form an envisage true to nature
  Through wind and rain
  They are monumentally structured.
  If ever god created a thing in need of love
  It must be a tree
  For humans have only two arms
  To long, to touch, to pray
  But trees have branches, growing out of branches
  Bowing to emptiness in life's roundelay.

THE EYES OF HEAVEN

This was in the beginning
   Before time skipped a beat
   Quite some time before
   He walked into my sleep.
   I'm sure you won't remember
   The final words he said
   Before the preacher
   Declared that my love was dead.
   My love spoke of many angels
   Who were coming for his soul
   He drifted in an out
   And finally lost control.
   I knelt by his side
   Trying desperately not to cry
   But the tears overflowed
   And this is how he said good-bye:
   "No more tears, no more tears
   God is coming for my soul
   I can see the stars coming
   Closer to the bed
   They are twinkling and sparkling

Inside my head
And my dream
Is coming true.

I am destined to shine
And guide you.
Make a wish on me
Make a wish on me."

Tonight and every evening
A chain of stars light my way
Their eyes rejuvenate my spirit
As night turns into day.
My love is a star in Heaven
Drifting in the arms of space
And one day we will be together
In another time and place.

THE FINAL STAGE

The light shines through the face of the clouds
   The blue is clear in your translucent eyes
   The showers cannot blind this heavenly embrace
   The tears cannot stain this crystallized face
   Bear not the pain, close not the mind
   Teardrops are falling, leaving me blind
   But always I can draw from you, from love.
   If by chance your balloon is released from captivity
   Do not place blame upon fate or destiny
   Reaching your bubble might cause it to break
   Bursting your bubble would be a fatal mistake
   For even the clouds are jealous of the chained
   Too free they are, travelling unordained.
   Trace the photograph outlined for the child
   Destiny searches for the meek and the mild
   Fill in the empty faces with a few forgotten phrases
   Duplicate and then proceed.

SONG FROM THE SEA

It was easy then
  To wander
  Aimlessly
  Without a worry
  Or anything
  To question your existence
  Or break your bubble.
  But then
  I came
  And everything around you
  Appeared to be untrue
  And unjust
  And you felt differently
  And you tried to mould me
  So that I
  Fit into your place
  But it was not to be
  It was too difficult
  To find a path
  That kept us together
  When we were both walking

On thin ice.
One could go
One could stay
It was easy then
Before you let me go under
For the third time.

THE PAINTER WHO WOULD NEVER BE

Colours called out
  To him
  In the night
  Arthritic
  Unsteady
  Old
  Unsure
  He tried
  In vain
  To create
  A masterpiece
  To live on
  After he had gone
  Instead
  Worlds collided
  Sea and sky bled together
  Smiling lady cried
  Bumbling
  Stumbling

Slipping on
Palette
Paint
Body
One.

Brush
Painter
One.

The sun rose
in peace and serenity
As he walked
toward
The edge
of the mountain.

He flowed
off the paintbrush
Into the open arms
Of the sea
Where he became
The painter who would never be.

BEAUTEOUS SUNSET

Beauteous sunset
   Coming down to greet the sea
   Heavenly father
   Reaching out to the free
   Living pictures,
   Grasping eternity
   Colours dancing
   Winding paths
   Going who knows where
   Spinning clouds
   Coveted by the wind
   Resonant diamonds
   Sing the night away
   Darkness silhouettes
   The garden moonlight
   All are reticent
   Calm and serene
   This is the miracle
   The miracle of nature.

   Moments are spent

Days are spent
Years pass
And still you dream your life away
Why must you dream
When nature is calling you to come and play?

BOYS WITH TOYS

When the world is coming apart at the seams
   And we're all looking for an answer to come through
   Listening to the boys threatening with their toys
   Toys that could annihilate both me and you.

   I stand at the foot of the flowing river
   Longing for a voice, a voice of common sense
   The arms of the wind hug me ever so tightly
   As I shudder at the man's impotence.

   History gave to the world men and women
   Leaders who used pens instead of swords
   Great writers who weren't afraid to speak out
   To put what was right on the records.

   Dickens, Longfellow, Emerson & Thoreau,
   They were men of peace they spoke for one and all
   Where are the leaders, the poets of today?
   It is to them I am making this call.

   For the leaders of the world are in crisis

I fear the future - not mind but my son's
We need someone to stand up to take control
Instead of boys with weapons and with guns.

Who are you poets of the year 2003?
Who are you? Where are you hear my cries!
Speak up now or forever hold your peace
This poet anxiously awaits your replies.

ONE OF THOSE DAYS...

Ever have one of those days?
  You know the ones
  When no email comes in
  And you've answered'em all from yesterday
  And you wish for snail-mail
  But the mailbox is empty
  Except for a Pizza Hut flyer

  Ever have one of those days?
  You know the ones
  When the past just won't stay down
  And either will breakfast
  Lunch or dinner
  And you keep hoping to be rescued
  But you're not sure what from

  Ever have one of those days?
  You know the ones
  When a magpie on the clothes line
  Watches you, like a long lost friend
  Someone you met once, a spirit in your life

Trying to get a message through
And you wonder who sent it to you

Ever have one of those days?
You know the ones
When someone cuts you off in traffic
And you want to read them the riot act
And you decide not to because life is too short
Besides, it might be someone you know
Deception lurks behind the tinted glass

Ever have one of those days?
You know the ones
When the page remains empty
And your only desire is to fill it
But your mind stays all a-jumble
Today I'm having one of those days
Have you ever had one of those days?

THE ART OF PARENTING

Children are the very mirror of your life
What they know, what they learn is from you
You worry about your foundation, it causes you strife
'Cause all your parents taught you, is what NOT to do.

Please remember that children live in every moment...
   Click-Click-Click go the cameras in their minds
To them life is a candy-store where days are spent
Opening wrappers, making choices of all kinds.

God gives parents a blank canvas: a child.
When you paint unconditional love comes through
The parenting rainbow connection - them to you.

Life is short, your time is well spent
Perfecting the artistry of a parent.

STEAMY

My love and my miracle, mine all mine
How you have altered my existence
Your life and my life, they are entwined
Daily you display your munificence
Filled to the brim and raring to go
I push your buttons, that is my desire
For 45 minutes, fast, faster, then slow
Steam rises, up, up, higher and higher
You are silent then, in all of your splendour
With each day I love you more and more.

In all of this world, it is you that I prefer
There's nothing like a fine dishwasher.

THE ICY HAND OF TIME

The icy hand
Of time
Steals sand
From my child.
He sleeps now
Calmly
Innocently
Peacefully
Sometimes he
Turns to me
And cries
Or moans
In pain
In his sleep
He reaches
I caress
We do not touch
We join
In spirit.

Often
I wonder
If he knows
That the
Hourglass
Is filled
With his
Lifeblood
And it is
Descending
In double time.

I pray
That one-day
He will
Come home
That one-day
I can hold
My child
For now
This glass coffin
Is all he knows.

SONG OF AUTUMN

The leaves crunch under my feet
   A snap crackle pop in my mind
   Rising, falling - soles kiss the ground
   Memories swirling around and around.

   The leaves were fragrant and musky
   We piled them up to the sky - sky high -
   A city girl's straw. We jumped yelling "Jeronimo!"
   They were as soft as virgin snow.

   Autumn took us into its arms and held us, lovingly.
   Seasonally. We were autumn children.
   We came alive – when the leaves began to fall
   Our spirits deciphered Mother Nature's call.

   The leaves are gathering at my doorstep waiting
   My sisters and brothers have come to call
   The spirit of autumn lifts me from the wheelchair
   We all dance together in eternity's autumn fair.

THE CIRCLE: A TRILOGY

A MESSAGE TO MY UNBORN CHILD

Child, child of mine
   Protected from the world
   Safe within my womb.

   Child, child of mine
   Unseeing and unknowing
   The world's state of doom.

   Child, child of mine
   You are me.
   I am your mother.

   Child, child of mine
   I am you.
   I will love you like no other.

   Child, child of mine

Peace. Pray for peace.
Time cannot heal all sorrows.

Child, child of mine
Peace. Pray for peace.
You are hope for all tomorrows.

Child, child of mine
Heart beating, limbs forming
You are unborn, the innocent one.

Child, child of mine
You are my hope for the future
You are the future, for everyone.

THE CIRCLE A TRILOGY:

GOOD NIGHT LITTLE ONE

Heaven isn't far away
   That is where he's gone to play

Dancing upon a cloud so light
   Dazzling all as he takes flight
   The tiny spirit who lived in me
   Now his soul has been set free
   My womb is empty, he is no more
   And yet I am not as I was before.
   Seeing him, lifeless attached one
   The end of life only just begun.
   Surrendering, child no longer mine
   In Heaven, eternally divine.

THE CIRCLE: A TRILOGY

TINY ANGELS

Shhhhhhh.
  Listen.

I hear them singing

  Listen.

  Can you hear them too?
  Listen.

  Their voices
  Are filling up my heart.
  It is so full
  I fear
  It might burst
  Within me.

  Listen.

Stop what you are doing and
Listen.

Trust me.
He is there with them.

Listen
With all your hearts and souls.

Listen...
Shhhhhhhhhh.

THE MARRIAGE PRAYER

When the photo in the frame cracks
And the wedding vows slip the mind
When only the memories are on track
And tears of unhappiness leave you blind
Then perhaps you must walk away
Turn your back on everything that you know
Perhaps it is time, you have tried it all
And still you feel somewhat hollow.
Before you leave and pack your bags
TALK to the one you love, reach out
Open up your heart, your soul to him
And perhaps you can work it all out
Too often we give up and move
When we only think we've done our best
If love was there, it can grow again
Even after it has taken a short rest
Now I'm not condoning staying with abuse
In that case to other horizons you must go
But if you think your relationship has use
Then let your heart lead and you follow
For the world is lonely and cold

Without someone with whom you can share
And remember you are getting old
And someone right beside you does care.
So start again, take romance from the shelf
Breathe life into a relationship that's stale
You won't regret it, do it for yourself!
True love can never ever fail.

BEAU IDEAL

Beauty never calms
   Those who cry
   Beauty never warms
   A cold good-bye

   When the heart is bleeding
   The ego needs feeding
   And beauty is no alibi
   For it never calms
   Those who cry

   When you are in love
   Beauty is everywhere
   When you are out of love
   The only beauty is in despair.

FATHER AND SON

Father teaches son to be a man
   Son teaches father to be a child again
   Together they walk hand in hand
   Watching them to me is so grand
   The two of them are magic at play
   Watching Thunderbirds on Saturday
   Father worries, can he be the man
   His child idealizes, sure he can.
   For his child sees he is strong and warm
   And will protect him from every harm
   Wouldn't disappoint him for anything on earth
   Father loved him long before his birth
   Father teaches son to become a man
   That is how it has been since time began.

FLEETING

And I shall pass
   By you like a breeze
   And will not touch
   Or leave a trace
   That I had been
   Only the sweet scent
   Of daisies and clovers.

FORGET ME NOT CHILD

Forget me not child
Of the golden field
Let them fall
And the message will be revealed
Do not use your petals
To hide the tears
Do not shield yourself
From their sneers
For your beauty is too great
To ever be concealed
Forget me not child
Of the golden field.

HANDS

Hands
We must cherish
Hands
To hold
To reach
Too cold
To teach
Hands
Moving over pages
Over bodies
Innocent caresses
Hands
Held
Promises broken
Fingers
Now unchained
Boxes
Filled with
Broken circles
Hands

We must cherish
Hands
Empty
Hands
Wrinkly
Hands
Reaching
Hands

Ideas flow
From these hands
Cherished always
Are the hands
Of an artist.

HE LOVES ME

HE LOVES ME NOT

There grew a flower
   It was springy new
   I picked the flower
   To see if our love was true
   I plucked its petals
   And tore it all apart
   While the picture developed
   In my hopeful heart.

   There on the velvet grass
   The dead flower remained
   And as the queen of hearts
   I rained.

IGNORAMOUS

I lost you in tomorrow
   A yesterday not past
   I closed my eyes in sorrow
   And before a moment passed
   Love disappeared, you with it
   Never would have thought it
   Could happen to one such as I
   The least you could have done
   Was bid me a proper good-bye!

PUT A BANDAID

I put a band aid on your puzzle
   After your pieces scattered everywhere
   I was your life jacket
   When you overturned in the sea
   I mended your broken heart
   Shattered beyond repair
   I pulled you up, lifted you
   From the depths of despair.

   Now I'm hiding in this tree house of imagination
   Seeking out kindness and guidance
   Asking no one, who will mend me?
   Asking the air, how can this be?

   I made you my mission, my good deed for the day
   I took all of your sadness away
   In return you ripped my heart in two
   Now it feels like I'm wearing cement shoes
   And I'm lost in a crowded emptiness
   Wandering, seeking what I cannot find
   Asking no one, who will mend me?

Asking the air, how can this be?
Asking, never knowing
Why?

IF I COULD...

If I could
   Turn back the hands of time
   I would make you mine
   For all of eternity

   You were my umbrella
   On a rainy day
   When you smiled
   All of my troubles faded away
   I lived and I breathed
   For you.

   You whispered your sweet lyrics
   Of love into my heart
   And I became strong
   And special
   And free
   All because
   You loved me
   And the sun, shone through
   When I became one with you.

But like a melody
Your love
Faded away
And all that was left
Was the constant repetition
Of a song that keeps playing
Over and over again
And won't let go
Of a mind.

If I could turn back
The hands of time
I would make you mine
For all of eternity
For all of
Eternity.

MIRROR MIRROR

Mirror mirror
On the wall
Will you catch me
If I fall?
Mirror mirror
What will you do
If the pieces shatter
And darkness becomes you?

Mirror mirror
On the wall
Can you tell me why
My reflection is so small?

ORGAN GRINDERS

Crawling along
The dismal hall
Putrid purple
Gruesome green
Smelling the stench
Of dead meat rotting
Human flesh
Dying
Obscene.

Seeing the old woman
Straddling the bedpan
The young man dead
Yet breathing
In rhythm
With the sound
Of the drip.

And through the love boat
Window

A man is butchered
While a monkey
Jumps upon his back
And someone
Wearing white
Tosses a single coin
Into his cap.

REFLECTIONS IN A MUD PUDDLE

Hazel green eyes
   Narcissistic view
   Of an underwater palace

   Pensive
   Yet empty
   Speaking volumes
   Of self
   To self

   Reflection
   Does not entirely
   Resemble
   Its viewer.

   Deep within
   The murky waters
   Protected from
   Faults, pain

And memories

Turning
Liquid pavement
Into a grimace
Reflecting a smile.

SHACKLED TOGETHER

Water falls
   From my mouth
   Into your bucket
   Rose petals
   Have already
   Been sifted
   Melting process
   Division necessary
   Reasons
   The same

   Installation of fear
   Arrives prior to
   The receiving
   Of the truth serum
   The baptismal rites
   Finally seem relevant
   But the pushing away voice
   Combination
   Joins and then divides
   Separation inevitable

It seems we have been
Shackled
Together here
For a lifetime
But you have only just spoken your name
I hear you
Screaming
In the night
Yet I cannot reach you
The abyss is
Far too great.

SIGN OF THE TIMES

Something is making crazy
   It is driving me around the bend
   Something that is so unbearable
   That I might even give up this friend.

   You see he is forever jibbering
   Yacking away, 24 – 7
   Doesn't matter if we're alone
   Or shopping at 7-11.

   Everywhere we go, it happens
   And his attention is diverted from me
   He goes off into another world
   And I am with him, and yet lonely.

   I keep wanting to say THIS IS IT
   I can't, I won't take this anymore.
   You have to choose, who will it be?
   It would be me who'd be walking out the door.

You see, I am a green eyed monster
A jealous bitch who deserves to be alone
I know when I'm licked, I just can't compete
With the ringing of his cellular phone.

THE ANSWER

You wear a mask
  All of the time
  I can't see you
  Disguise isn't a crime
  My lonely heart
  Keeps telling me
  That you could be
  The answer.

  You wear a mask
  Black and blue
  You are lost
  In a Halloween hue
  I wait
  In anticipation
  You just can't see
  That you could be
  The answer.

  If I asked you
  To remove it

To show me
Who's behind it?
Would you laugh?
And taunt me
Knowing that
I must be lonely?
I stand before you
Wanting to know you
Still you cannot see
That you could be
The answer.

DEATH OF A SNOWFLAKE

The snowflake turned into a tear
   It died instantly
   Never made a single sound
   They fall from the sky
   In the shape of a star
   And can only survive
   Until the sun comes alive.

   Water, water everywhere
   We step on them without a care
   Nothing was, and nothing will be
   Do not cry for destiny.

THE PAST

Soaring like a vulture
  Over my shoulder
  Smirking
  Endlessly
  Swooping
  When necessary
  Often
  Seeming to be
  A friend
  Vulnerable
  I am
  You are
  An enemy
  Stop lurking
  I am not ready
  Get off my back
  Dragging me
  Down
  Let go of
  The past.

THE UNSPOKEN

Beautiful sunrise
  In my heart
  Spectrum of colour
  Magnificent art

  My mind rests
  On your shoulder
  Brown eyes on blue
  Everything that I am
  I am, for you.

WATERMELON LADY

I was a bird
Once
But didn't like the freedom
When I saw how far
I could fly
Without getting tired
In a seat, on a plane
I yearned to be a
People
They seemed
Strong and logical
And I admired how
They tried to
Improve themselves
Whilst I flew in circles
Carried by gusts
And watched my babies
Starve
In the spring.

And that is how
I came to be
A watermelon lady
Planting and sowing
Gathering and selling
Sleeping away
Half the day
Working for pittance
And watching my children
Starve all year round.

I was a bird
Once
And didn't like
The freedom
And now that is
What I long to be
Instead of a
Watermelon lady.

I was a bird
Once
But didn't like
The freedom,

The grass is always greener
The grass is always greener
That's what they always say
I'd rather be a bird again
Instead of a watermelon lady.

HEARTLESS

To take you
  Into
  The palm
  Of my
  Hand and let your
  Heart
  Run through my
  Fingers like
  Sand
  Mixing with
  The other abominations
  On the beach.

To place you
  Inside a
  Mail packet,
  Seal it up and
  Then mail you
  To some
  war ridden country
  C.O.D.

With no return address.

To put you
On display
In a glass
Encasement
And charge
Per view
While everyone
Pokes sticks
At you.

Then I would
Rescue you
Capturing your heart
Only to
Crush it again.

PASSOVER

Like a piece of paper burning in a fire
   Like hatred turning into desire
   Like a river with no reason to tell the truth
I lost my youth.

Now I am old and grey
My beauty has wrinkled away
And many dreams have been lost
All at cost.

Now I walk out into my garden
As a valley of violets beckon
Their fragrance guides me along
Nature and I never so strong.

Looking bare-eyed toward the sky
I see a rainbow horseshoeing its way
All around droplets of rain sing
The emerald grass is shimmering.

My soul is yearning with no regrets

Toward heaven like steel to a magnet
Whispering fountains it seems
Serenade my journey: Sweet Dreams.

TAKEN TOO SOON

(WRITTEN AFTER HEARING THE NEWS OF THE MURDER OF JOHN LENNON)

And when I could no longer stand
  YOUR LEGS became mine.
  And when I could no longer cry
  YOUR TEARS became mine.
  And when I could not find myself
  YOUR IDENTITY became mine.
  And when I could no longer believe
  YOUR PURPOSE became mine.
  And when I could no longer speak
  YOUR WORDS became mine.
  And when I could no longer live
  Your death BECAME MINE.

WHISPER

Whisper, whisper I am whispering
This secret is mine only mine
I alone can make my heart sing

No matter what kindness you bring
My spirit seeks a different sign
Whisper, whisper I am whispering

Sometimes a lesson is heart-breaking
Sometimes you are pulled into line
I alone can make my heart sing

Enchained by your golden ring
In your comfort zone you recline
Whisper, whisper I am whispering

My soul wants to soar on golden wing
Up there the world will be mine
I alone can make my heart sing

And yet I do not reveal a thing

For the unknown can be sublime
Whisper, whisper I am whispering
I alone can make my heart sing.

SCARAMOUCHE

His picture
   Lacking substance
   Is framed
   By unnecessary splinters
   From his soul.
   Fragments
   Once bled
   With a fight
   Are now given freely
   Reflecting
   Self-contempt.

   CHORUS
   Let us not
   Allow the wind
   To blow him over
   Let us rebuild
   Where reality has
   Opened the floodgates
   Let us make him
   Whole again

Let us give
Him purpose.

Scaramouche, is revealed
The truth cannot be concealed.

CHORUS
Let us not
Allow the wind
To blow him over
Let us rebuild
Where reality has
Opened the floodgates
Let us make him
Whole again
Let us give
Him purpose.

WALKING DOWN THE PATH

Walking down the path
   Toward The Taj Mahal
   Society was building trees
   Preparing for the fall.

   Chapels were opening their arms
   To the new world in prayer
   They use to seek the word
   From a reliable soothsayer

   Then mirrors eyed the eyes
   Which were too blind to see
   The birth and the origin
   Of creativity.

   Now a painter paints a waterfall
   And no one asks him why
   Because we understand it all
   Is for a spirit in the sky.

This is the new millennium
Where translations come for free
We share our lives on-line
Creating a sense of community.

We were all born citizens
On the wings of a dove
The answer has always been ours
In one word it is love.

BARRIER

Barrier separating
  Walls breathing
  Formaldehyde droppings
  Poisoning minds
  With bits and pieces
  Savior
  Kaiser
  Of all buns
  Barrier dividing.

  Melt the air
  With words
  Of encouragement
  Mushroom clouds
  Are not for human consumption
  Why break through
  When you can
  Break down?
  Reflections of a
  Troubled prostitute
  Reading a biblical passage

Examining the remaining days
Of his life
Whore-monger
Of the universe
Words take flight
Like a bat in the valley
Of death
Flapping
Entrapped by a
Misunderstanding
Misrepresentation
Melt the air, melt.

Barrier
Separating
Melt with
Words of encouragement
Dividing one
One in the same.

I drift
From one thought to another
It doesn't matter
No one knows
And time is endless
Yet slips away
And nothing gets done
And memories only chain me
In this futility
Even more.

Someone is screaming
(or is it me?)

Tell them to shut up
(why am I screaming?)

A bird is singing
On my window
I focus all of my life's energy
Onto it
And when it flies
So goes my spirit
Out into the endless blue
Which I once
Took for granted.

SLIGHT MISUNDERSTANDING

Throwing caution to the winds
   The youth withdrew his gun
   The man behind the counter shook
   The boy promised he'd harm no one.

   The child escaped into the street
   Like a single cloud in the sky
   He never felt the agony of defeat
   Now did he hear the sirens cry

   Because a policeman just off duty
   Shot him down in self-defence
   Nipping it in the bud, courageously
   One more death in the sea of violence

   His badge radiated in the sun
   There was no pulse on the boy
   Carefully the knight lifted the gun
   It was only a child's toy.

MACBETH

When you come down from your mountain
To my computer by the sea
A data processing I will be; numbers.

Listen to my keyboard
Blocking out reality
Click clacking music
No need of identity

You hated your boss
You seized the moment
Started a mutiny
Now you sit
Upon his throne
Sending GIC's down
To paupers who are paid
To punch punctually
By the sea

A hunting you will go

For what
I do not know
But when you find it
You know where I will be
A data-processing
By the sea.

PERHAPS

Perhaps
  The symphony
  Is playing
  too loudly
  Tears
  Are forming
  In my eyes
  I hear
  a choir singing
  In my mind
  There are lyrics
  Being sung
  But the words
  Have not yet
  Been written

  Perhaps
  My imagination
  Is playing
  Tricks
  on me again

You are
serenading
Me
With a
symphony
There are no words
And yet
The words
Reverberate
In my mind.

SIPHON

A priest will raise his collar
   To hide from what exists
   A razor into the cold will cut
   To siphon bleeding wrists
   A tiger will pounce upon the heart
   Ripping the Samaritan apart
   No one said good
   No one told me that you were
   But you were damn good
   Of that I am perfectly sure

Now you fly into space
Breathing upon the glass
Frost paralyzes your face
Brains amputate the past
Tell the whole world
Because they want to know
Tell them how you sold your soul
For poison in a needle.

UNANSWERABLE LETTERS

I wrote to you
Because the sun shone
In this rainy mind
Whenever I remembered your smile.

I wrote to you
Because I missed you
I missed your laughter
And most of all your gentle touch.

I wrote to you
Because you held my heart
In the palm of your hand
And I believed
No matter how far apart we were
You would always be here with me
And I with you.

I wrote to you
Asking for all of eternity
But it had already gone
And the letters melted before I could send them

I never wrote to you.

BUTTERFLY

Monarch butterfly
  Gathers up into the air
  Momentarily pausing
  Then lifts without a care.
  Its colours flow freely
  Like paint onto a canvas
  Its wings embrace the sky
  In casual serenity:
  Beauty in motion.

  Dancing on a flower
  With utmost delicacy
  Unconsciously it flaunts
  Its superiority
  Fluttering like a ballerina
  It climbs toward the sky
  I yearn to be as free as
  The monarch butterfly.

EVOLUTION

Snowflakes fluttering into the eaves trough
Whispering messages to travelers below
Evergreen combs brush the flakes away
Covering the earth with a blanket of snow

It was a shallow evening in late December
A time that I would rather not remember
When angels fell down to this very earth
Sent by the master to determine our worth

Cleansing images reflected in the pool
They fed and clothes each and every fool
We danced until all of the stars came down
And the trees inherited a golden crown

Time flew, and more dreams were spun
The angels painted smiles upon everyone
Until all the worth sparkled and was bright
Glowing with the power of a celestial light

We sang aloud, one church one song
And the non-believers joined to make us strong
When the lord gathered souls, some were not called
They were born into nature, and a new world evolved.

THE WORLD IN 60 SECONDS

(DEPENDING ON HOW FAST YOU READ)

Foot in mouth
  Tongue in shoe
  Satellite
  TV too
  Harry Potter
  Welcome Back Kotter
  Caught in a time warp
  No place to go
  Watching death match
  Blow by blow
  Elevator muzak
  Druggies stoned on crack
  Rolling Stones
  Kate Moss

Nailing Brian
On the cross
Trains collide
Computers crash
Hi-tech
Star Trek
Mouth to mouth resuscitation
Out and out discrimination
Judge Judy
Live to work
Tutti Fruity
Work to live
Too blind to see
Must see to believe
Rapping Christianity
Exposing virginity
Teletubbies in the know
Mourning the Seinfeld show
Flowers Flowers
Kensington Park
Joan of Arc
Lips that burn
Teeth that grin
Children born
Free from sin
Ozone layer
Dragon slayer
T-Rex
Same sex
Sex sells
Talking on cells
Flapping wings
Flying skies
Catching waves

Mickey D's fries
Wal-mart
Heart to heart
Walking on the moon
Mooning strangers
Out of the frying pan
Also ran
Dancer dances
Dressed in free
No one seems to notice
Except the emperor and me.

GOSPELAMER

The spider crawled toward
   The powder blue sky
   Spinning in a cloudy web
   Which took years to comply

   When nearly at his destination
   The old and graying spider
   Without thinking out the situation
   Tried to web it wider

   Whirling far too carelessly
   For one in his golden age
   The angel called immortality
   Took note of his page

   To the gossamer he was chained
   Fate threatened his masterpiece
   Then by a miracle it rained
   And he slipped to his release

   It rained for forty days and nights

Seemed there wasn't a trace or mark
Just one old and graying spider
Webbing his way onto Noah's Ark.

Acknowlegements

Dear readers,
 Thank you for reading this collection of my poetry. I wrote my first poem "The Beginning" when I was in High School. Poetry has always been my first love.
 Thank you also to my parents, to whom this book is dedicated and to my grandmother who was a poet in her own right.
 Thank you to my dear friends who embraced my wordy nerdy aspirations.
 And thanks to those who helped me with putting this new book together. I couldn't have done it without you!
 As always,
 HAPPY READING!
 Cathy

About Cathy

Multi-award winning author Cathy McGough
lives and writes in Ontario, Canada,
with her husband, son, their two cats and one dog.
If you'd like to contact Cathy please send her an email to:
cathy@cathymcgough.com.
She loves to hear from her readers.

Also by:

FICTION
Everyone's Child
Ribby's Secret
Thirteen Short Stories (which includes: The Umbrella and the Wind; Margaret's Revelation; Dandelion Wine (READERS' FAVOURITE BOOK AWARD FINALIST))
Interviews With Legendary Writers From Beyond (2ND PLACE BEST LITERARY REFERENCE 2016 METAMORPH PUBLISHING)
Plus Size Goddess
NON-FICTION
103 Fundraising Ideas For Parent Volunteers With Schools and Teams (3RD PLACE BEST REFERENCE 2016 METAMORPH PUBLISHING.)
+ Children's and Young Adult books

Milton Keynes UK
Ingram Content Group UK Ltd.
UKHW022158260624
444643UK00007B/76

9 781998 480142